Making Space For The Divine

Insights of a Modern Mystic

Peter Mulraney

Copyright © 2023 by Peter Mulraney

All rights reserved.

No part of this book may be reproduced in any form or by any electronic or mechanical means, including information storage and retrieval systems, without written permission from the author, except for the use of brief quotations in a book review.

ISBN: 978-0-6458829-3-3

Cover image from photograph taken by author.

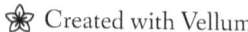 Created with Vellum

To Toni, who keeps me grounded in the reality of living the human experience.

Contents

Introduction	vii
Making space for the divine	1
I'm a mystic, not a guru	3
You don't need to be religious to be a mystic	5
The path to enlightenment	7
The art of keeping a journal	9
Conscious living	12
Answering the call	15
Two ways of entering dimensions beyond the physical	17
The power of storytellers	20
Changing a cultural story	25
Take control of your story	29
Trusting the process of life	32
Hearing the voice of God	35
The pursuit of happiness	37
Scripture and cultural evolution	39
Creative nothingness	44
It's time we had a talk about fall-redemption theology	47
Atheists, fundamentalists, and mystics	52
Power: We all have some	56
Choose to love anyway	59
Nothingness	62
It's a shame Jesus didn't write a few things down	64
Love one another	68
The power of hindsight	71
3 Self-healing practices for busy people	74

Living alone: An opportunity for self-discovery	77
Letting go of things	79
Grief and grieving	82
A note from Peter	85
Also by Peter Mulraney	87

Introduction

This is a curated collection of articles (originally published on petermulraney.com or Medium.com) exploring insights I received while pondering things from the perspective of a modern-day mystic living in the world.

This is not a book to be read in one sitting or in any particular order. The insights presented here are an invitation to reflect on your assumptions about life and your beliefs about the divine. That's not something to be tackled lightly, but it is a task you'll need to undertake once you start on the voyage of self-discovery I refer to as the mystical journey.

Introspection is not something we're used to doing in our busy lives but, as I have discovered through exploring the process over many years, spending time examining the assumptions and beliefs underpinning your behaviour and outlook on life is life changing.

In reality, the only thing you actually need to change is your mind - but you need to know what's in your mind before you can change it - and introspection will help you with that.

Introduction

I hope you find these insights helpful as you take a few quiet moments to delve into some introspection during your busy day.

Peter Mulraney

Adelaide 2023

Making space for the divine

Nothing shows up in your life unless you make a space for it.

If you want a special person in your life, you need to make space for that relationship. Let's face it, you're not likely to attract that special person into your life if every waking moment of your day is already taken up by work, sport, and social commitments.

Something has to make way to allow that person in for your relationship to flourish.

It's the same with the divine.

If you want a relationship with the divine, you need to make it a priority and that means making space for it in your daily routine.

The most common excuse I hear whenever I suggest to someone they take up meditation or any other spiritual practice is: I don't have time to do that.

Would that be your response?

In the field of personal productivity, we talk about the difference between being busy and being productive. Being busy is simply filling your time with activity. Being productive is engaging in focussed activity - tasks aligned with a productive objective.

In my experience, you can be busy and non-productive, and you can be productive without being busy. It comes down to how you choose to use your time.

If you want to develop a relationship with the divine but don't think you have time to meditate or pray, make a list of all the things you spend your time doing. Then, declutter that list.

If you're serious about developing a sense of your spirituality, you need somewhere between twenty minutes and an hour each day.

When I started on the mystical journey, I simply got up half an hour earlier each morning so I could meditate. Over time, I started watching less TV and spent more time reading and writing in my journal. Then, I gave up a few weekends to attend retreats away from home. The more time you make available to the divine, the easier it becomes to allow the divine into your life.

The secret is choosing to make it a priority.

Works every time, whether you're making space for the divine, a relationship, or your life's work.

I'm a mystic, not a guru

Like all mystics, I acknowledge the presence of the divine and make space for it in my life.

Although I share my insights and discuss the tools I use, I don't tell you what to believe or how to live your life. If that's what you're looking for, you'll need to find someone else.

What I do is invite you to examine the way you live your life and question the beliefs you were taught. In other words, I invite you to awaken from the sleep of inculturation.

I call making space for the divine The Mystical Journey. St John of the Cross called it The Dark Night Of The Soul. The author of *A Course In Miracles* claims it's a required course we all get to take - eventually.

There are days when I feel like a monk sitting in a cell in a monastery, because that's how it works. Yes, modern mystics are called to engage with the world, but we also need to make space in our lives for being in the presence of the divine, and that requires time in silence, whether it's sitting in your room or walking in nature.

I've reached that time in life where I can spend my day alone with God if I choose, but in the thirty plus years leading up to this point, I chose to make time for the divine every morning before engaging with the world to earn a living. These days, my engagement with the world is through my writing and my social life, and the occasional talk about my writing.

The mystical journey doesn't require activism, even if it sometimes leads you there. It's more about allowing the presence of the divine into your life and listening to your inner guidance before doing anything. I know I'm not going to solve the world's problems by writing about them but there are times when I feel called to make a suggestion or to amplify the message of more informed activists.

But the mystical journey is not about escaping into some spiritual dimension and ignoring what's going on in the world. We're here in the flesh for a reason. If it was simply about being in the presence of the divine, we would have stayed in the Heart of God and not bothered with incarnating in a body to live a life on earth.

I think it's safe to assume engaging with others in the world must be important in the greater scheme of things. Perhaps it's about raising awareness.

It's obvious from what's going on in the world that not every soul on the planet is aware of itself or awake to the presence of the divine. There must be a reason why things are the way they are.

Perhaps there really is great joy in the return of the lost sheep.

You don't need to be religious to be a mystic

In fact, it helps if you aren't.

Being a mystic is a spiritual pursuit, not a religious one.

I started on the mystical journey after becoming disillusioned with religion, and that took some time. I needed to work through a long transition to disentangle myself from my religious upbringing. If you're facing a similar challenge, take heart, it can be done.

Religion gives you certainty: a set of beliefs presented as the truth. Religion works through doctrines and rules for living. It is the safe highway. You don't have to think for yourself. All that's required is following the rules. Salvation is guaranteed - as long as you live within those rules.

Becoming a mystic requires moving beyond rules and doctrines and finding your own truth. It requires a leap of faith and moving through the fear that you're putting your salvation at risk by stepping off that safe way your religion provided.

Spirituality is what happens when you start looking for your connection with God in places beyond the rules and safe havens of religion. When you shift to spirituality, you work through your direct connection with the divine.

Spirituality is for grown-ups - the people prepared to take responsibility for their lives.

If you want to play it safe, stick with religion. Millions have.

If you want the truth, set out on the mystical journey. That's where the excitement is.

Being a mystic isn't the same as being secular. Mystics know there is a God and incorporate their spirituality into their everyday lives. That's why they're into service and social justice.

Being a mystic is not about sitting on the mountain top. It's a call to be engaged in life.

Becoming a mystic might be just what you're looking for.

The path to enlightenment

> *Enlightenment: a clear understanding of who you are and your place in the great scheme of things.*

The path to enlightenment is not what you think it is.

If you're anything like I was when I started my search for enlightenment, you probably think you need some special technique or secret knowledge to attain it.

Maybe you're under the impression you need to spend years meditating or doing yoga to get your chance at enlightenment. I was.

But, it turns out you don't have to sit on a cushion, go on a ten day silent retreat or do anything like that. You don't even have to leave home.

In *The Jeshua Letters*, Jeshua reminds us of a simple truth.

> '*Your moment-to-moment experience is the path to your enlightenment.*'

In other words, the divine reveals itself through the mundane; the divine acts through the ordinary; the divine is in the moment-to-moment experience of your life.

If you want to see it, pay attention.

It's easy to live life without paying attention, which is why most of us live that way.

When you're not paying attention, you blame everyone else or God when things aren't working out for you. I've been there. It doesn't get you anywhere. It certainly doesn't lead to enlightenment.

If you want to understand who you are and where you fit into the great scheme of things, study yourself - not the life of some so called holy person.

Give it a go.

You'll be surprised. You'll uncover your patterns and realize you can change your lived experience by changing your mind.

You'll dissolve your masks and meet yourself, which is how you allow enlightenment into your field of awareness.

The art of keeping a journal

The practice of recording your intimate thoughts in longhand.

There is something about writing down your thoughts on paper with a pen that doing it with a computer doesn't replicate. Maybe that something will fade into oblivion along with handwriting as the digital age progresses. Perhaps it's nothing more than a sense of nostalgia for the slower times of the pre-digital analogue age. Maybe young people no longer feel it. I hope I'm wrong about that.

I learnt to write longhand a long time ago, when it was taught in schools everywhere, back in the days when none of us had ever dreamt of, let alone heard of, a computer. Over the years I even took time to master calligraphy, the ancient art of hand lettering, so maybe I am yearning for the trappings of a lost age that's long gone.

You don't need to go as far as learning calligraphy to keep a journal but, if you do, you'll acquire an ability to make beautiful marks on paper. You might even turn your journal into a work of art resembling a medieval manuscript. At least you'll be able to read it twenty years from now.

I will continue to record my thoughts and insights by hand in a journal for as long as I can. Writing down my thoughts, and those insights that pop into my awareness after meditating, allows me to capture them, which gives me an opportunity to come back and reflect upon them later.

If you don't write them down, your thoughts and insights become like those dreams you forget about as soon as you wake up. In my experience, an unrecorded insight is usually lost forever.

If you use a journal to record what you think about each day, you get the chance to discern the patterns in your thinking. If you simply record what you do each day, you get to identify the patterns of your activity.

I journal in the morning, but many practitioners of the art journal at night as a way of reflecting on their day. There are no hard and fast rules about when is the best time to journal, but there is one suggesting daily as best practice.

A journal is a place where you can try out ideas or spell out your dreams. It's a safe place for designing your life or having an ongoing discussion with your higher self. The contents of your journal don't have to be made public unless, like me, you use it as a place for developing ideas into articles to be shared as insights from a crime writing mystic or expanded into a book.

Speaking of books, journals can serve as source material for memoirs if you are inclined to share your life story, and biographies, if someone else thinks your life is interesting

Making Space For The Divine

enough to write about. Hopefully, you will no longer be on the planet by the time someone else gets around to reading your journals for that purpose, unless you've authorised the writing of a biography in lieu of penning your own memoir. Of course, there is always the option of destroying your journals before you die or leaving instructions in your will to that effect.

If on the other hand, your handwriting is anything like mine, worrying about what others might read in your journals will not be a concern, as long as you stay with handwriting and don't give in to the temptation to replace your pen and paper exercise with a computer.

You don't need a special notebook to keep a journal - any exercise book will do. But, if you're looking for something a little more substantial, there are purpose designed journals available, including a few designed by me.

Conscious living

Conscious living: being aware of who you are, where you are, and why you're doing what you're doing.

This is not how most of us start out in life. We are born into cultural stories and told our cultural story is the truth about how things are in the world and the universe.

What you get told is the truth, however, depends on where you're born, which religion your parents belong to, the ideology of the local governing elite, what they teach in the schools you attend, and who controls the media you're exposed to.

Our cultural stories are exclusive. They teach us about us and them, where the 'them' is anyone living outside our cultural norms. They also let us know who is in charge and what laws we have to follow. But, those same cultural stories tend to entrench the powers of existing elites and keep the rest of us subservient.

Making Space For The Divine

None of our cultural stories are true. They are all made up. Their purpose is social cohesion and control.

As long as you don't question the reality of your cultural story and live within its confining boundaries, you continue to believe what everybody around you believes is the truth of their reality. You remain trapped within the belief bubble of each group you belong to: family, political party, religion, nation etc.

Conscious living is how you live life once you wake up from the dream of your cultural story.

To wake up, though, you have to question everything you have been told and decide what to believe for yourself. You need the courage to look outside your cultural story. You need to be open to new information, to putting aside your religious framework and discovering your own spirituality, and living life from your new state of awareness.

In that new state of awareness you'll have an expanded understanding of who you are and why you're doing the things you choose to do. You'll become more aware of the people around you and what they're doing to influence what you think and how you behave. You'll also start to perceive new possibilities and opportunities for working with others and solving some of today's problems.

The decision to wake up and live consciously is empowering but it comes with some challenges. The power figures in your life often feel threatened when you start questioning their authority and the level of control they exercise over your life. You come under pressure from friends and family to stop the madness and stay the same as everybody else. You'll be tempted to fall back into the herd - but there is no going back.

New friends and new possibilities beckon once you awaken from the dream of your cultural story.

Answering the call

It's not unusual for people to think being a mystic requires answering a special kind of calling to devote your life to God. After all, if you read the lives of the saints - the so-called holy men and women of history - you get the clear impression that's how they understood it. And, they often retreated into seclusion in monasteries, convents, ashrams or caves to live out their special calling.

There are people who still see it that way. But, being a mystic is no longer restricted to such special people. Today, you don't need to be a saint or even holy to be a mystic.

A modern mystic is someone who makes space for the divine in their life. And, that space is what makes the difference. There is no longer a need to retreat into seclusion. You can be a mystic right where you are, no matter your circumstances.

I believe we're all called to be mystics, even if it's often difficult to hear the call. There's a lot of noise in the world. There are a lot of distractions, and we often want to be distracted, since it's not often we want to be honest with ourselves. So, while we're all called, we don't all answer. Some of us don't hear the invitation. Others don't want to or consciously choose not to. That's the power of choice or free will.

We are living in what are called secular times, where the influence of the major religions is waning. People are drifting away from organised religion, disenchanted by preaching that doesn't resonant and behaviour which is contrary to the very rules they have been urged to live their lives by.

But, after walking away from their religion, a lot of people find themselves searching for something - they're just not sure what it is.

That sense of knowing something is missing in your life, that wanting to know who you are and what life is really all about. That's the call. That's the divine calling you to the mystical journey.

Don't think you have to be in a post religious world to hear that call. The divine calls everyone, including those who continue to pursue the religious life.

When we hear the call, some of us throw ourselves into changing the external world - saving the planet, alleviating poverty or fighting corruption. All good causes, but ultimately distractions from answering the call.

Those who answer the call discover the mystical journey, and come to realize they first have to put their inner life in order, before they can effectively change the external world in which they are living their human life.

Two ways of entering dimensions beyond the physical

The story we're being sold through the media is not about reality. The camera may not lie - although that's a debatable question these days - but someone selects the images we see, someone even decides which images get captured, and someone writes the words used to tell us the story. And, it is a story we are being sold. It's never objective reality. It's always someone's interpretation - often coloured by an unspoken agenda.

The media, whether it's mainstream or alternative, deals with events in the surface world. We live our daily lives within that surface level dimension, where we engage with the world and the people around us. While it's important to know what's going on in the world we live in - family, neighbourhood, workplace, nation - the surface world is not the only dimension available to us.

We are connected to invisible dimensions beyond the physical.

We're here to play in the physical world, otherwise we wouldn't be here at all. But, we never actually leave the spiritual, although we tend to forget it while we focus our attention on the physical - until someone or something reminds us of our connection. Then, it becomes impossible to forget, even if we lose our sense of connection again.

We journey into those non-physical dimensions through meditation and sleep.

In meditation, we make the journey consciously. We choose to go there because we remember our connection. In sleep, we journey into those dimensions unconsciously. We go there whether we choose to or not, whether we remember our connection or not.

Some of us don't enjoy our nightly journeys into the non-physical. We have nightmares. But all of us need to go there, as anyone who has experienced insomnia can tell you. Sleep is an important part of waking up, since it's the one state of being where the ego mind is not available to block communication from the divine.

Meditation - sitting and allowing the mind to empty or sitting and watching thoughts go by without engaging with them - allows you to temporarily remove your attention from the physical and connect with those parts of yourself that reside in the invisible, those divine aspects of yourself not caught up in the drama of what you call your life in the physical.

Whenever what's going on in the world all gets to be too much, slow down. Take a moment for yourself and meditate.

Making Space For The Divine

If you can't meditate, have a nap. You can always come back to the drama later - if that's what you really want.

By the way, it's a good idea to sleep and meditate daily to promote health and well-being - and stay connected to the divine aspects of yourself beyond the physical.

The power of storytellers

We're all storytellers. We use stories to define who we are and to explain the world. We use stories to answer questions, justify behaviour and predict the future. But, even when we believe our stories are true, there is no guarantee they are.

Some storytellers make up stories for their entertainment value. We all enjoy a moment of escape from the realities of life, so who can blame them for making up a few distracting yarns? Entertainment, after all, is a form of community service we all appreciate.

The world would be a different place if storytellers were confined to the field of distraction we call entertainment. Such an arrangement would make it easier to tell the difference between the illusions of their stories and reality. But, as I'm sure you already know, it doesn't work like that.

There is no escaping stories or storytellers. There is only retelling, editing and rewriting, and the birthing of new stories - for without new stories, there is no way out of the old stories.

Personal stories

We tell stories about ourselves, and everyone we know tells stories about us. There is usually common ground across our stories, indisputable facts that hold them together in a coherent retelling of the events of our lives. Things like the date and location of our birth, the names of our parents and siblings, where we lived, what schools we attended, and our position in the family structure.

Yet, despite all the common details, the stories we tell ourselves about ourselves do not always align with the tales others tell about us. Often, we can't even agree with the versions of the story of our childhood retold by our siblings, let alone the ones told by our parents or teachers. Presumably they were there as witnesses or participants in the events we remember, even if their memories generate stories that differ from our own.

So, whose story can we trust or believe as being a retelling of the facts as they really happened? Let's face it, none of us has a perfect memory, so maybe none of the stories of our childhood are true, not even the ones we tell ourselves. Maybe today's children will have a better go at sorting out their memories thanks to their digital records - but, I doubt it. We now know that pictures can lie.

And, what about those stories we use to define who we are? Is there any truth in them?

We all grow up within a cultural context. And, what's a cultural context if it's not a multilayered story of who we are as the people who live the way we live?

Cultural stories

We are social beings. We live in groups. Every group has a defining story, some of which are thousands of years old. But, it's not only indigenous cultures that are living examples of ancient stories. The defining stories of western civilization, what we in the West like to see as the modern world, are also rooted in the ancient history of the Greco-Roman world.

Cultural stories are based on assumptions and mythologies. They represent the agreements people have struck for living together in groups. Over time, some of the mythologies change. We no longer believe in the gods the Romans or the Ancient Greeks worshipped, for example, but a lot of their assumptions appear to have had a long shelf life.

We're still defining ourselves in exclusive ways, dividing ourselves into separate groups and regarding some as others or the enemy. Like the Romans, we still believe that might is right and it's okay to impose our beliefs and way of life on anyone who stands in the way of what we decide is progress.

Cultural stories also provide the context within which we construct our personal stories. In other words, the very concepts we use to describe who we are, whether to ourselves or anybody else, are defined by the beliefs and language of our family group, a subset of the larger cultural group into which we were born.

This is why people with exactly the same values, wanting exactly the same things out of life but living in different parts of the world, can see each other as different and even be convinced they're enemies.

And, it's not just people living in different parts of the world that can be turned into the enemy. Anybody living in our society that doesn't belong to our political, ethnic or racial group, worship our God, or support our team can be turned into an enemy by story. Storytellers are that powerful.

It's time for a new story

The internet is disrupting cultural stories. Despite the efforts of power elites in some places, people all over the planet are interacting in real time, and it's difficult to see ordinary people in other countries as different or the enemy when they're sharing common stories and giving voice to common aspirations.

It's also difficult to hide anything now that anybody with a smartphone and an internet connection can upload a video or tweet a post as soon as something happens anywhere in the world.

The internet has given a platform to alternative views, which are challenging the stories of entrenched voices. Yes, some of it is misinformation from those who want to maintain the divisions that give them power and advantage. Some of it, though, is myth-busting information that threatens the status quo.

We're all storytellers. Each of us can participate in the telling of our cultural stories and change the narrative to birth a new story of a more inclusive world. We can birth a story about caring for our planet and every living being. We can help each other transition from the old story of division and destruction to a new story of unity and wellbeing.

Peter Mulraney

Once a story is told, it takes on a life of its own. Storytellers are that powerful.

Changing a cultural story

I've been reading *The More Beautiful World Our Hearts Know Is Possible* by Charles Eisenstein. It's got me thinking.

If Eisenstein is right, what our hearts know doesn't align with what our heads tell us about the world. Our hearts know about love, generosity, sharing, inclusiveness and gratitude. Our hearts know on some level all forms of life on the planet are connected and what you do to one you do to all. Our hearts know we are part of the global ecosystem.

Our heads don't see it that way. Our heads tells we are the dominant species and everything on the planet is a resource to be exploited for our benefit.

We've been telling ourselves that story for thousands of years. We've built civilizations on it. We're even using it to justify exploiting the resources of space and spending billions preparing to send people to Mars.

But, something is not right.

Anyone who's paying attention to what's happening in the world knows something is not right, even if they don't yet want to admit it or know what to do about it. And, it's more than climate change. It's more than inequality. It's more than the rampant destruction of forests and wetlands. It's more than oceans of plastic. It's more than the insanity of nuclear weapons. It's more than thinking we can wage war to solve anything. But, it incorporates all those things.

The story of separation

According to Eisenstein, the root cause of our current dilemma is the story of separation - the story we tell ourselves about being special and different from other groups of humans and other forms of life on the planet. This is the story that allows us to dehumanise people that look different, speak a different language or believe in a different God. This is the story that enables systemic racism and the rape and pillage of the planet in the name of progress.

If this story of separation is so destructive, why does it persist? Why don't we do something about it?

The short answer is: Our culture is built on it. It's the story that defines economies using concepts like scarcity, competition, and survival of the fittest. It's the story that defines political systems as a battle between progressives and conservatives and delivers government by elites. It's the story that divides people into groups according to the colour of their skin and what they believe.

It will not be easy to break out of the story of separation. We're immersed in it. The media keeps repeating its mantras to us every day. We teach it to our kids because we think it's the story of the way things are and we want to prepare them for life in the world.

We don't even know it's the story underpinning our way of life until someone like Charles Eisenstein comes along and brings it to our attention, and then it's obvious. So, what can we do about it?

Changing a cultural story

Changing a cultural story is no easy task. The story itself determines the questions that get asked in our discussions. We need to become aware of alternative stories if we are to insert alternative questions into those discussions.

A first step is becoming aware of being inside a story. And, we are inside the stories that make up our cultural story. That's simply the way things work. You can't not be within a story because that's how we're initially taught about the world.

When I started my own journey of self-discovery, I started with the religious story I had grown up with. I questioned what I had been told, explored other stories and told myself a new story based on what I experienced. I've done the same with other stories - about money and the economy, politics and politicians, success and failure, love and fear.

When we realize we are inside a story, or using a story to explain how things work in our world, we can change the story when it no longer aligns with our reality.

Changing a cultural story is a massive undertaking but it is underway in many parts of the world. In some places it will invoke revolution. In others it will bubble up from the expanding awareness of people like you and me.

If you want to be part of this evolution, start with examining the stories you're living your life by and asking whether they're your stories or somebody else's. Test their assumptions against your reality. Be brave, explore alternative narratives and join in the conversation. Pay attention and wonder why when you hear about people protesting in the streets. Question statements made by political leaders and commentators, since every person in a position of power has an agenda, and that agenda does not necessarily include your best interests or the good of the nation.

If you're interested in exploring how you can participate in changing our cultural story, reading *The More Beautiful World Our Hearts Know Is Possible* by Charles Eisenstein might be a good place to start.

If you're interested in starting on a journey of self-discovery through reviewing your personal stories, *My Life Is My Responsibility*, from my portfolio of books, might be a good place the start.

Take control of your story

If you listen to the news media or spend your days scrolling through social media posts, it's easy to fall into the trap of thinking the sky is falling. It's not.

If you're finding the news depressing; turn it off.

If you can't trust what your friends and others are sharing on social media; do your own research or stop reading the fake news posts they share.

In your life, you are the main character.

Your life is about you and you are the author of your story, even if you're inadvertently following someone else's script.

To resume control of your story, all you need to do is accept responsibility for deciding what's important in life and what it means for you.

It's easy to let media experts, political commentators, and politicians tell you what's going on in the world - and to blame them for the mess we seem to be in. But the reality is, they're all only bit players in your story. In your life, you are the main character. The story is about you and you get to tell it from your perspective.

The challenge is to discern your authentic voice from all the others you hear within your mind, which you can't do unless you're prepared to examine the content of your mind.

To become aware of what's going on in your mind, stop listening to the external voices of the world and start listening to what you tell yourself. Pay attention to what you hear yourself say and think, and, if you can, write it down.

A daily practice of reflecting on the events of your day and keeping a journal of your thoughts will help you become aware of what you believe about yourself, the people in your life, and the circumstances of your existence.

Unfortunately, a lot of what we tell ourselves is not true but, unless we question what we say about ourselves and the world we live in, we'll continue to believe it.

One of the challenges we face living in a media dominated world is taking on the opinions of people we regard as experts, while failing to recognise that every commentator has an agenda that does not necessarily align with what's in our best interest.

There is only one person who can decide what's in your best interest - and that's you.

Only you get to walk in your shoes.

Since the day you were born, a lot of people with the best of intentions have told you what's in your best interest. The

Making Space For The Divine

reality is, though, parents, teachers, and friends can only give you advice from their perspective.

Only you get to walk in your shoes. Only you get to see things the way you see things. It's not possible for anyone to understand your lived experience the way you do.

To control your story, you have to work out what's in your best interest every time, and that means putting aside the opinions embedded in your cultural, religious, and scholastic education and determining what the facts are, and what they mean for you.

And, the best thing about being the author of your own story is you can edit the details and change the storyline. You can even reinvent yourself and start a new story.

Trusting the process of life

Allowing yourself to experience life as it unfolds requires forgoing all pretence of control. In other words, allowing life to unfold entails trusting the process of life.

Yes, you can voice your intentions, dream your dreams, and work towards your goals. You can make plans. But, despite your planning, you only ever get to take the next step towards your desired destination from within the context of your understanding of reality.

Yet, even with the best of plans, there are no guaranteed outcomes.

Life unfolds as you take the next step and wait to find out what happens. And, no matter what happens, you only have control over your response to that outcome and deciding your next step in light of your new circumstances.

You can dream and scheme as much as you want, but life only unfolds one step at a time according to its plan. The challenge is learning to align your dreams with life's plans.

Making Space For The Divine

Sounds impossible, I know. But, there are things you can do to facilitate aligning your plans with life's.

- Pay attention to what happens in your life as a result of the steps you take.
- Wonder why things happen when they do - and, remember, things happen for you and not to you.
- Become aware of the beliefs and assumptions that guide your decision making.

That last one is vital, since if you're not aware of why you make certain decisions, you'll keep making them - even if you don't enjoy the outcomes they bring.

An unpleasant outcome is life's way of telling you to make a different decision, since all outcomes are consequences of decisions made. To make a different decision requires changing your mind but, to change your mind, you first need to be aware of why you made the original decision. In other words, you need to live consciously if you want to benefit from life's lessons.

Living consciously is being aware of what's going on in your mind and circumstances while you are trusting the process of life.

We are not talking about living in blind faith. We're talking about paying attention to what life is telling you before you take your next step. We're talking about adjusting your plans to align with life's feedback, instead of blindly blundering on because you think you know what's best for you.

None of us has all the information or a full understanding of the bigger picture. We only see the world through our little window - and, often, our little window needs a clean before we can see clearly.

Hearing the voice of God

Ever wondered what the voice of God sounds like? Do you imagine it would be like someone whispering in your ear? A voice you'd hear inside your head? Or are you waiting for a great booming voice from the heavens - like in the movies?

If you're still wondering, you probably haven't heard it, yet. Or perhaps you have, but didn't recognise it for what it was.

One of the problems with expectations is they create illusions - things we imagine will confirm our expectations. When you expect God to speak in a particular way, you're on the lookout for that voice. Anything else you might hear doesn't make the grade by your chosen standard.

Trouble is, though, God's voice has many forms, including the full range of sounds you can imagine, and forms with no sound, for example, when God speaks on the breeze or through feelings that stir the heart.

But, there is a challenge to hearing the voice of God in all its forms: noise. And, that noise is both internal and external.

Our world is full of noise, especially the noise of the marketplace, where everyone is clamouring for our attention. It takes a lot of effort to hear your own voice, let alone the voice of God, when you're constantly bombarded with distractions.

The noise of the marketplace is external. You can shut it out by turning off your devices and disengaging from media and conversation. You can retreat into your sanctuary, that place where you go to get away from it all. You can even go on a formal retreat and withdraw from family, friends, and obligations for a period of quiet reflection.

But, even in those periods and places of quiet, there is still noise: the internal noise inside your head. That voice that never seems to shut off. You know the one. Your inner voice.

The secret to hearing the voice of God is learning to silence your inner voice. That's what's really meant by going into the great silence of prayer or meditation.

The funny thing is, once you find that great silence, you can go there no matter where you are, even if you're standing in the marketplace surrounded by noise.

The pursuit of happiness

Chasing happiness? Stop it!

The pursuit of happiness, as most of us understand it, is a futile undertaking. It leads to addiction and exploitation as we attempt to find whatever it is we think happiness might be, which most of us appear to confuse with pleasure.

Happiness is not something you can capture or find outside yourself. It's a feeling you choose or an attitude you adopt. No-one can give it to you except yourself and, likewise, people can't take it away from you. You don't need to pursue it. You only need to express it.

From a mystical perspective, happiness arises from allowing life to unfold without resistance or trying to control everything and dictate outcomes. It's an attitude that allows you to go with the flow of the river of life instead of determinedly paddling upstream against it.

The pursuit of happiness, on the other hand, is driven by our desire to have things go our way or our desire to be in control. But, it's an illusion, or maybe even a delusion, to think you can actually control things or manipulate the process of life. Of course, this hasn't stopped us from trying, has it?

But instead of happiness, mostly we find frustration and disappointment when we try to control life. So, why do we do it?

I suspect the pursuit of happiness comes from a misunderstanding of the term in this line from the US Declaration of Independence

> "We hold these truths to be self-evident, that all men are created equal, that they are endowed by their Creator with certain unalienable Rights, that among these are Life, Liberty and the pursuit of Happiness."

I don't believe the framers of the declaration meant the pursuit of pleasure when they wrote those words. I suspect 'the pursuit of happiness' was how they worded their idea about having the right to make a better life for yourself.

Making a better life for yourself is a different ballgame. It's got nothing to do with pleasure but with improving the circumstances in which you live. Interestingly, this works best when we work together to build a better world for all of us - instead of adopting the narrow focus of only making a better life for ourselves.

Scripture and cultural evolution

I often wonder how much the intended meaning of the texts regarded as sacred scriptures has been lost or distorted through the process of translation.

Let's face it, none of the books of the Bible, for example, were written in English. The English language didn't exist at the time they were written. In fact, none of the scriptures of the world's major religions were written in English. We're all reading translations, and as someone who is bilingual, I'm acutely aware of the pitfalls of translating ideas expressed in the words of one language into the words of another. Word choice is everything when it comes to conveying what the translator understands as the meaning of the words being translated.

And, how many of those ancient texts have lost their significance through the evolution of ideas since they were written? To be honest, I suspect we need to be open to the possibility that all of them have suffered some loss of significance, and some of them more than others.

From my perspective, it's arrogant to regard scripture as the inerrant word of God. That's a claim. Not a fact, since all scriptures, not only the books of the Bible, were written by mere mortals - whether we believe they were inspired or not.

Scripture can be said to be the word of God only in the sense that it was authored by people imbued with the divine essence of being - people like you and me, and every body else on the planet. From that perspective, you could rightly claim that every written text is the word of God, including this one. But that's not what those making the claim about scripture being the word of God intend. Their intention is to justify their beliefs and behaviour. Their intention is to make them right and you in need of conversion.

If you care to read the English translation of your scriptures, it's not difficult to appreciate that their authors, and subsequent translators, were influenced by the cultural norms and knowledge of their times - and we're talking about authors writing under the influence of worldviews from several thousand years ago.

But, in case you haven't noticed, there have been a few changes here on the planet since Adam was thrown out of the Garden, Moses was wandering around in the desert, and Paul was penning his letters to the Corinthians. Quite a few changes, in fact, as any student of history knows.

Cultural evolution is an on-going process. In the last century alone, we have witnessed tremendous cultural change and an explosion of knowledge in all fields of study, and that's on top of the advances made in the Age of Enlightenment and the Renaissance. Talk to your grandparents about how things have changed over their lifetime if you need a little more insight into what I mean. The scope of the change has been breathtaking for those of us who have lived through it.

Scholars assign the writing of the most recent books of the Bible to the first century CE or the first century AD for those still using the old terminology. That means they are two thousand years old, and they're the most recent books in the collection. Think about that for a moment. What do you think those authors would make of our world? I'm guessing they'd be somewhat confused and more than a little surprised that we're still reading their words.

Now think about the advances in medical science in your lifetime. If you suffered a heart attack, would you want to be treated by a doctor trained in one of today's medical schools or by one relying on the medical knowledge written down by his colleagues in the time of Augustus Caesar? I'm guessing you'd choose the doctor who washes his hands and uses sterile equipment, modern anaesthetic, and antibiotics - the doctor using the latest medical science.

We could work through examples from every field of knowledge but I'll spare you the tedium. I'm sure most of us would prefer to work with practitioners employing the current best practices of their field and not with those relying on the practices their predecessors used in the Middle Ages or before.

Okay, I acknowledge there are some exceptions in the fields of several manual arts, like calligraphy, for example, but even modern calligraphers, who employ the same skills as their predecessors, use metal nibs and acrylic inks, and modern scripts. But, in the main, our world is very different to the world of our scripture writers.

So, why do some of us insist on claiming the truth can only be found in their translation of scriptures written thousands of years ago? From my perspective, there's a level of arrogance in making that claim, and perhaps a little insanity. We've stopped relying on the ideas and knowledge of the ancients in many fields, yet some of us still insist on the reliability and accuracy of the knowledge of the writers of ancient scriptures.

We do not look at the world in the same way that the authors of the books of the Bible and other ancient sacred texts looked at the world in their time. We have different perspectives. We know, for example, more about our place in the universe, thanks to the Hubble Space Telescope and our obsession with space travel. The writers of the Old Testament thought God lived in the sky above the clouds - up where the International Space Station orbits.

There is truth in scripture, but it's not literal truth. Scriptures are teaching stories. They were written by people of faith or by people wanting to codify beliefs and behavioural norms. They are products of their time and they are not the last word on anything. They're out of date and often make little sense to modern readers.

It's arrogant to think any scripture contains the inerrant word of God or that God stopped speaking to or inspiring people some time in the first century CE.

Only those who want to limit what you believe make that claim, and you are not obliged to listen to them. You don't need their permission to question their assertions. You only need a little courage and the willingness to discover new answers to age old questions.

Making Space For The Divine

God speaks through many voices and in many languages. As someone who makes space for the divine and asks questions, I've come to realize that God speaks to all of us - and not only through the words of scripture.

Creative nothingness

Modern science demands empirical evidence from proponents of an idea before entertaining the possibility that what is being proposed has a shred of credibility. Yet, modern science entertains the idea that the universe began with a big bang and that all life evolved from the output of that bang through a series of random events.

If you think about it, the big bang theory proposes the creation of the universe from a creative nothingness. After all, something had to trigger that big bang which showered the universe with stardust. In other words, the universe and everything in it is a manifestation of an indescribable nothingness.

That indescribable nothingness sounds a lot like that which Lao Tzu termed the Tao, and what mystics of all faiths call the divine.

The body may be made of stardust, as astrophysicists are wont to tell us, but like every other living thing it also returns

Making Space For The Divine

to dust when it dies, while whatever animated the body returns to the nothingness from which it arose.

The difference between those living according to the beliefs of science and those living a life of faith is that those living a life of faith allow for the possibility of the divine. They allow for the existence of spiritual dimensions beyond the senses of the body, beyond the known physical world. That's why it's called a life of faith.

Those adhering to the logic of the rational scientific mind believe they are their bodies and that life ends at death. For them, there is nothing beyond the physical universe so there is no possibility of an afterlife.

People of faith believe they are spirits or souls with bodies for the purposes of being human in the physical dimension and that death is a transition into the spiritual, a return to the divine or creative nothingness from which they came into physical reality.

Mystics believe life has a purpose beyond the physical dimension. The evidence generated by human activity, however, suggests that the rational scientific mind believes the purpose of human life is to bring about the destruction of all life on the planet - fossil fuel induced global warming, plastic pollution, destruction of habitat, and warfare are a few of the things humanity seems determined to pursue despite their cost to life on the planet.

When we listen to the voices of indigenous cultures - something we haven't done for a long time in the rational thinking West - we hear them saying the same thing as the mystics - that life is filled with the energy of the creative nothingness and all living things are connected in a web of life that dances to the music of the divine.

Science gives us the technology and knowledge which underpin our current lifestyle but the rational mind of science is closed to the mysteries of life, to the creative nothingness which manifests as the universe and everything in it.

Mysticism provides a pathway to the creative nothingness which is the ground of all being, and is open to anyone interested in the mysteries of life.

It's time we had a talk about fall-redemption theology

Fall-Redemption theology is a pretty weird line of thought when you think about it. For a start, there are two fall stories - each set in a different dimension - wrapped up in this theology.

The first is the story of Lucifer, which turns an archangel into the devil, Satan, and involves the creation of another dimension or place cut off from God: hell.

The second is the story of the fall of humankind, which starts with the story of Adam and Eve being kicked out of the Garden of Eden through the agency of Eve and the actions of the devil, who has somehow managed to insert himself into God's creation in the physical dimension.

This second story progresses to the story of Noah and the ark, and God's first act of redemption - a cleansing by way of a flood and a starting over through the offspring of Noah. Unfortunately, this doesn't work out as planned and leads to the Tower of Babel, where God intervenes (again) to create division and confusion through language in an effort to thwart our ancestors' attempt to reach the heavens. That intervention eventually leads to the Hebrews, through the agency of Abraham - who needs a little help from the divine to impregnate his legal wife in order to start the line of descent - although he's had no trouble getting his maidservant pregnant to start an alternative line, but that's not part of this story.

Then we get another redemption event through the agency of Joseph, wearer of the multicoloured dreamcoat, who rescues the Hebrews into Egypt only for them to fall into slavery, so Moses (with divine assistance) can redeem them again, and lead them into the promised land.

The redemption story celebrated at Easter

By the time we get to the events that the Church regards as 'the redemption' story, which we celebrate at Easter, the Hebrews in their promised land are once again a subjected people, this time living under the rule of Rome. But, this redemption story is set beyond the physical world, even if it plays out in events firmly set in the physical dimension.

In fact, this story links back to the first fall story, the fall of Lucifer, which reputedly initiated the war between the forces of good and evil, and led to our fall into sin through the actions of Adam and Eve. This last redemption story is about God intervening directly in human affairs by inserting 'his only begotten son' into humanity - for the express purpose of allowing him to be sacrificed to atone for all of the errors stemming from the first fall and to set things right in God's creation.

Making Space For The Divine

In the physical story, if we can believe the gospels, we see the rich and powerful in a backwoods of the Roman Empire do what the rich and powerful do everywhere - silence a voice of dissent. They kill a troublemaker, named Jesus of Nazareth, using the most horrific means available to them: crucifixion.

What happens next is intriguing, and has been occupying the minds of scholars and believers for centuries.

Immediately after the crucifixion, stories of resurrection emerge, though they aren't written down for years and they can't be verified.

In the years after the crucifixion, we not only have stories of what Jesus was reputed to have taught his disciples but explanations of the significance of his life, death and resurrection aligned with the Jewish prophecies of a redeeming Messiah, thanks to the authors of the writings we know as the New Testament.

And, finally, centuries later, we get the Church, a group of people who teach these stories as if they are divinely inspired truths. These are the people that come up with fall-redemption theology to explain it all, despite the fact that none of the originating stories of their theology can be authenticated.

The God of this theology doesn't even align with the God Jesus is reputed to have spoken of - the God of love or the God described as a loving father who loves his children unconditionally. So, why have we bought into this theology, this story, for most of the last two thousand years? And, why are so many of us, now that we are literate, walking away from it?

As Christians, we want to believe we have been saved from sin by the act of a redeeming saviour. That's the message we've been given as the good news. We want that 'get out of hell for free' card. I understand that. But, I'm left asking a question: If Jesus' death and resurrection represent the triumph of good over evil, the vanquishment of the devil, how come there is still so much evil in the world today?

It doesn't take much research to realize that on the world stage, nothing changed after Jesus' supposed act of redeeming sacrifice some two thousand years ago. The Romans went ahead and destroyed Jerusalem and lots of other places. European nations arose from the ashes of the Roman Empire and went on to conquer, colonise and exploit most of the countries on earth. Warlords, emperors and kings everywhere carried on with business as usual, through two world wars, right up to this day where they are still killing unarmed voices of dissent.

What's the value of this fall-redemption theology?

I don't see any real value in believing this theology. It's nothing more than a salve for guilty consciences, a false promise that no matter how you live your life, you're saved as long as you acknowledge Jesus as your Lord. It's a great excuse for self-righteousness.

However, this theology has value as a weapon of power for those who claim to speak for God. The Church, for example, has been playing the power games of empire ever since it became mainstream in the 4th century CE. In other words, thanks to Constantine, the Church became another vehicle through which the rich and powerful could exert control over the masses, and the message of fall-redemption theology has been pretty effective at keeping us in line until recently.

Today, most of us in the West can read, and when people read, they start to think for themselves.

Time for a more personal theology.

It's time to realize you're the saviour you have been looking for. No-one's getting a free ride into heaven because someone, unknown and unrecorded outside the words of the New Testament, was crucified in Judea some two thousand years ago - despite what's been claimed about him.

It's time to wake up to the reality of this being your life and you being responsible for how you live it.

To develop a personal theology, make some room in your schedule for allowing the divine into your life. Like anyone else you want to get to know, God will remain a stranger unless you spend some quality time together.

And, take it from me, once you do that, you'll discover there's no falling or redemption required.

Atheists, fundamentalists, and mystics

Every one of us is somewhere on the belief spectrum. Whether we're willing to publicly acknowledge where we sit on the spectrum is a personal decision. It may be that where we sit is a movable feast - the precise location depending on the circumstances of our lives.

Atheists, fundamentalists, and mystics occupy three clear points on the belief spectrum. There are others but we can use these three to explore the scope of the spectrum.

Atheists

The non-believers. According to atheists, there is no empirical evidence proving God's existence and the current state of world affairs is more than enough evidence to demonstrate that there is no all powerful being in the heavens.

Atheists are people that question everything, not just the existence of God. They tell us they're rational thinkers, that they only believe in the facts.

Their perspective is derived from the physical world in which we live. If something can't be seen, smelt, heard or touched it doesn't exist. If it can't be measured, it's non-existent. They place their faith in their ability to explain the physical world. There are no psychics among this lot.

They're resigned to this life being all there is and ceasing to exist at death. They don't believe in an afterlife. That would require a leap of faith beyond the physical realms known to them.

Fundamentalists

The true believers. They believe what they've been told about Almighty God - literally. For fundamentalists, their holy book is the unerring word of God. They do not question the doctrines and teachings of their religion. These are the people that claim to know the will of God and to speak in His name.

And, like the God they speak for, they're judgemental. They know what's right and what's wrong. They're not much into fun and they're definitely not into sex, unless it's for procreational purposes within the confines of the sacred union of a marriage blessed by their religion.

Fundamentalists have certainty of belief and like to tell the rest of us how to live our lives - especially if we don't want to spend eternity in what they call hell. They believe in the afterlife and in that all powerful heavenly deity the atheists deny exists.

Mystics

The witnesses of the divine. Like the atheists, mystics question everything, especially the scriptures and religious doctrines that give the fundamentalists their certainty. They realize God is unknowable from an intellectual perspective and are open to the existence of spiritual dimensions.

Mystics are not looking for empirical proof of God's existence or searching for certainty of belief. They're open to there being more to life than the physical dimension and one short lifetime stretching from birth to death.

For mystics, thinking and talking about God are distractions. They've learnt you need silence to allow the divine to reveal itself. Using meditation, mystics turn their attention away from the noise of the external world, the world of the ten thousand things, and allow the divine to make its presence known from within.

Mystics won't tell you what to believe or how to behave. They know you have to find that out for yourself.

Our default start point on the belief spectrum was determined by the cultural circumstances of our birth. Some of us never question the initial set of beliefs we inherited from our culture. That's how beliefs persist from generation to generation and become entrenched within a culture.

Others eventually come to question the beliefs they were born into and go in search of answers - and find themselves opening to new perspectives and moving to a different point on the belief spectrum.

I've moved from a starting point of Orthodox Catholicism - somewhere in the fundamentalist zone - to being a modern day mystic. It's an ongoing journey of self-discovery - a journey I encourage you to take.

Power: We all have some

Most of us, I suspect, are suspicious of power. After all, we hear of its corruptive influence often enough. You probably know the quote (or at least a paraphrase of it) attributed to Lord Acton:

> 'Power tends to corrupt, and absolute power corrupts absolutely. Great men are almost always bad men, even when they exercise influence and not authority, still more when you superadd the tendency or the certainty of corruption by authority.'

We all have the power of agency, the power to make our own decisions, which allows us to exercise control over our destiny.

Those of us living in liberal democracies have access to more power to make our own decisions than those living under authoritarian regimes - but we may not be as free as we like to tell ourselves we are. And, people living under authoritarian regimes probably have access to more personal power than the authorities have led them to believe. They just have to be more careful with how they exercise that power.

From an early age, we're encouraged to hand our power over to authority figures: parents, teachers, priests, policemen and politicians, to name a few. In fact, as part of the compromise of living in society, we've collectively handed significant power to the State in trust. We've entrusted our governments with the power to make laws regulating behaviour and property rights, which makes sense when you consider the implications of large numbers of people living together in the one place. It would be chaos if we didn't have agreed forms of behaviour and rules encouraging us to respect the rights of others.

But, as Lord Acton reminds us, we need to keep an eye on the people making the rules in our name. Sometimes they go too far and make rules favouring one group in society at the expense of all the others. Think about the way the tax laws, for example, tend to favour the interests of the wealthy while all of us wage earners are taxed at source on payday. Or think about the rules that stop businesses from making false claims in their advertisements, while there are no rules stopping politicians from lying to us. And, then, think about all the rules impinging on our rights made in the name of national security.

If we want to keep our freedoms and the power to choose, we need to be active in the political life of our societies.

It's not only the political arena where we need to exercise our personal power. We need to reclaim all that power we handed over to authority figures when we were young. It was appropriate for our parents to exercise control when we were children, but it's no longer appropriate now we're adults. We need to take back control of our lives.

I'm sure our teachers always had our best interests at heart, but they operated in school systems that pushed specific agendas that were not necessarily in our interest, and taught us things that are no longer true, even if they were at the time.

There has been an explosion in knowledge across the last century, especially in the fields of science, and some of that new knowledge has yet to make it into the textbooks.

And, let's remember, rote learning is not the same as critical thinking. It's high time we exercised our power to think critically about everything we encounter in life, especially about anything some supposed expert is pushing on social media.

And, what about the beliefs we were taught? Blind faith is not faith at all. It's the result of indoctrination.

We have the power to question what our elders told us was the truth, and we owe it to ourselves to do just that. That's why I wrote *My Life Is My Responsibility* - to encourage you to exercise the power you have to find out the truth for yourself and change your world.

There is no point in having the power to make your own decisions, if you refuse to use it.

Choose to love anyway

Is there continuity of life or awareness after death or does everything end? In other words, do you transition into a spiritual dimension or simply cease to exist? This is one of life's big questions.

Unfortunately, there is only one way to find out for certain. You have to go through the process. Anything we might tell ourselves in answer to the question beforehand is belief based conjecture.

All of our non-scientific sources of information on the afterlife are connected to either ancient sacred scriptures or channelled resources.

How do you verify a channelled resource, like *A Course in Miracles* or the *Way of Mastery* trilogy? Take it from me, it's not possible. I've studied both those resources. Either the message resonates with you or it doesn't. What the message does is challenge your beliefs but, in the end, you're still left with an act of faith when it comes to the source of the message.

Sacred scriptures have more credibility in the eyes of many, after all, they've been around for thousands of years, but that in itself is no guarantee of the validity of their content.

The whole religious endeavour is built on trust and our attempt to answer questions like: Is there a God or an intelligent being behind creation?

Our struggle to answer that question, which we've been trying to express ever since we were able to articulate our thoughts, is what generated the texts we now regard as sacred scriptures. Again, we're back in the realm of faith. If we believe what's in our scriptures, we're placing our trust in what people thought the answer was a long time ago - thousands of years ago, in fact. Not to mention the long line of people who have translated and interpreted those scriptures so we can read them in English.

And, let's not kid ourselves that science has the answer to the question. Science, which is all about explaining the physical universe, requires its own leaps of faith when it comes to explaining the origin and nature of life. We can study the body, but only up to the point of death, which means science has no knowledge of what happens to our life force beyond that point. As far as science is concerned, it ceases to exist when it can no longer be measured. Science can be described as a set of beliefs supported with evidence but, for most of us, believing what scientists tells us is still an act of faith, which is why we have so many conspiracy theories about vaccines, the earth being flat, and the moon landings.

Sometimes, I think the only way to feel the presence of God is to imagine it. At other times, it really does feel like I'm

Making Space For The Divine

alone in the universe, even when surrounded by millions of people.

Maybe the whole purpose of life is to enjoy it while it lasts, and not to worry about death and what, if anything, comes after it.

It's comforting to believe we all go home to God when we die, but if life ends with death, what is there to fear? If you no longer exist, what is nothingness but an abstract idea? It's the people who believe in a judgmental, vindictive God who have the most to fear - if they're right and haven't lived by their self-imposed standards. Happily, I'm not one of them.

From my perspective, it's better to live your life from love, even if it makes no difference in the end, since, in my experience, it makes for a more enjoyable life experience.

There is already more than enough pain and suffering in the world, caused by people acting out of fear or an overblown sense of self-importance instead of love. People that act out of love don't start wars or exploit their neighbours, they act with compassion and kindness. They understand we're all in this together and we're all going to die, no matter how much power or wealth we accumulate while we're here.

You can't take it with you, even if there is an afterlife. And, if there isn't, what's the point of having the most spectacular tombstone in the cemetery?

You don't have to believe in anyone or anything to live a life inspired by love. It's a choice you make every day, a choice to make the world a better place while you're here.

Nothingness

Some days it seems there is nobody there when you sit in meditation.

You start reciting your mantra or focusing on your breath. Your mind plays with a few random thoughts and, then, you come out of your meditation with a start, wondering what happened.

You know time has elapsed, since the display on your phone is telling you that it's twenty, thirty, or even fifty minutes or more later. But where have you been?

One minute you were there breathing or reciting your mantra and, somehow, now it's all those minutes later. What were you doing while all those minutes were streaming by? Did you go to sleep? Did your mind shut down? Did your awareness cease to exist?

It can be a bit disconcerting, especially for novice meditators, when your mind disappears.

Making Space For The Divine

When you start meditating, you expect to be aware of what's going on in your mind, even when it becomes still. But that's not what happens.

Most days your mind ticks over with random thoughts and you find yourself refocusing on your breath or your mantra as you become aware of those thoughts.

Some days you just watch your mind and marvel at the random nature of what it entertains itself with.

Sometimes you find yourself ensnared and wandering off the path chasing a thought down a rabbit hole.

Sometimes it's difficult to meditate because the mind is so caught up in the dramas of your everyday life and won't let them go, no matter how many times you refocus.

It's no wonder some of the masters refer to it as the monkey or puppy dog mind. It's interested in everything and it's easily distracted.

Maybe, that's why those days when your mind is quiet, or you're able to stop listening to it, that it seems like there is nobody there.

But someone is always there: you. You are the awareness that is always there watching, listening, and feeling whatever is going on inside and outside of you.

It's just that when the mind is still, there is nothing to be aware of - except the nothingness.

It's a shame Jesus didn't write a few things down

The form of Christianity I am most familiar with is Catholicism, since I was a practising Catholic into my fifties.

For the last twenty years, I've been what is known in Church circles as a lapsed Catholic, which means I usually don't go to Mass or participate in the sacramental life of the Church. It doesn't, by the way, mean I have given up on God. I have simply developed a different relationship with the divine within the Christian tradition.

For the last little while, though, since I started acting as chauffeur for my increasingly frail mother, I've been accompanying her to Sunday Mass. It's an act of service, and an opportunity to spend time with people acknowledging the presence of God in their lives within a supportive community.

When you have unlearnt the lessons imparted to you in your youth and opened yourself to thinking about God differently, it's interesting when you revisit what was once the familiar. It's also revealing to listen to the way in which the scripture readings are proclaimed as the word of God and how their meaning is explained. Once, I would have listened attentively to the lesson derived from the words. Now I listen and wonder why the Gospel writer chose those words to tell the particular story chosen for the day's reading.

Despite what is known within scholarly circles in the Church about how the Gospels were written, at the local level they're still spoken about as if they are historical records of the life of Jesus of Nazareth. They aren't. They're not the inerrant word of God, either.

The four books known as the Gospels according to Matthew, Mark, Luke, and John are teaching stories. They were written by people who believed Jesus was the promised messiah to persuade others of the truth of their belief. They're books of faith, not history. Their authors interpreted the events of Jesus' life in light of their faith.

No matter how you read them, the Gospels are not a complete or reliable record of Jesus' life and they were all written decades after the time period in which Jesus is thought to have lived.

From my perspective, the Gospels contain a collection of teachings ascribed to Jesus and a telling of his story in a way that makes it look as though he was the fulfilment of a string of Jewish prophecies. This latter aspect popped out for me in a Gospel reading one Sunday after Easter. The reading was Luke 24: 13-35; On the road to Emmaus. In particular, verse 27 caught my attention.

> "And, beginning with Moses and all the Prophets, he interpreted to them in all the Scriptures the things concerning himself."

I sat up when I heard that and thought, wow! That verse spells out precisely the main intention of the Gospel writers: to weave all the prophecies related to the coming of the messiah into the fabric of Jesus' story.

That's got to be a disturbing insight for anyone who believes in the historical record aspect of the Gospels. And, yet, I wonder how many people in the congregation that Sunday even noticed. I suspect all they heard was the literal meaning of the words as they were used in the story, like I used to before I started thinking about things differently.

In addition to the Gospels, the Church has a penchant for the writings of Paul. The opening chapter of Paul's letter to the Romans contains a specific declaration about Jesus being the Son of God; Romans 1: 1-6. This might explain why Christians started to worship Jesus as the Son of God, although the Jewish Authorities didn't acknowledge him as their messiah - despite all those fulfilled prophecies.

This led to Christians treating Jesus as a special divine being and claiming he died for our sins and defeated the forces of death and evil, all of which, to modern ears at least, sound both outlandish and unprovable.

It's a shame Jesus didn't write anything down, apart from a few doodles in the sand while he was waiting for those without sin to stone the woman reportedly caught in the act of adultery. John 8: 4-11.

Making Space For The Divine

I've always wondered about that story. Where was the man she was caught in the act with? Why isn't he being dragged into the village square to be stoned? But, I get it now. It's a teaching story, not an account of an actual event.

It's a story about diffusing your moral indignation by applying the law to yourself before you condemn another.

And, it's a story of acceptance told with these few words: neither do I condemn you.

Love one another

Love one another as I have loved you. John 13:34.

What does this really mean?

Let me start by saying it doesn't mean what you usually hear at church about giving up your life for your friends like Jesus did, which is the meaning associated with another version of this command: John 15:12–13.

Let's be honest with ourselves. Jesus didn't die for our sins or give up his life to let us off the hook. That's wishful thinking. You are responsible for the way you live your life. There is no 'get out of jail free card because Jesus died for your sins' in this game.

If Jesus died for anybody's sins, he died for his own—the same sins committed by all political activists or voices of dissent, and, in case you haven't noticed, we are still silencing people for speaking out against abuses of power.

And, killing them is only one of the options available today. Now we can destroy a person's reputation on social media, create fake news about them, deny them access to press conferences, or terminate their careers.

But, this is not what Jesus is talking about here. He's asking us to love as he loved. Not die as he died. He's not even asking us to be political activists. He's asking us to be loving people.

Jesus was someone who associated with religious leaders and prostitutes. He dined with publicans and tax collectors. He touched lepers and spoke to Samaritan women. In other words, Jesus was present to the people he was with and inclusive. He ignored religious taboos. And, when he acted, he did so with compassion and loving-kindness.

You might have to read the bible with an open mind to get some of this. You also need to be aware that Jesus lived in a time of religious intolerance, when the religious authorities in his community regarded both tax collectors and Samaritans as less than human, and it was against the religious laws to touch lepers or associate with prostitutes.

Jesus also reminded people of God's unconditional love in a time when religious leaders were interposing themselves between God and his people, and setting all manner of rules and regulations about how people should live their lives.

If you're not familiar with the concept of unconditional love, check out the story of the prodigal son (Luke 15: 11–32), and the one about the landowner who paid all his workers the same amount (Matthew 20: 1–16).

Jesus' words are an invitation to be present, to be inclusive, and to act with compassion and loving-kindness. His words are an invitation to act in ways that nurture peace and goodwill. Remember, he also asked us to love our neighbours as ourselves (Matthew 22: 39), and to love our enemies (Matthew 5:44).

His words are not a command to go out and get yourself killed for somebody else's sins. Millions of young men have gone out and done just that, and it still hasn't bought peace to our world, despite what we were promised by the leaders who sent them.

It's time we tried the approach Jesus asked us to emulate: loving one another.

No point in complaining about what our politicians are doing to foster division if we aren't prepared to love one another in our families, ours neighbourhoods, our country, or our world.

Love one another.

Sounds like a good idea to embrace to me.

The power of hindsight

Hindsight is an understanding of a situation after it has happened or developed. In other words, hindsight is making use of feedback from life experiences.

But, beware. Hindsight can be either a gift or a curse - depending on how you choose to use it.

Looking back when things work out.

When things go well, hindsight allows you to congratulate yourself for a job well done or a decision well made. Most of us have little trouble acknowledging and taking credit for our successes. When we use hindsight on events that went according to plan, we learn what worked for us and know we can use those behaviours or strategies again to our advantage.

Looking back when things don't work out.

It's when things don't work out that hindsight can either be a powerful tool for learning or for berating yourself.

For example, if real estate prices go down over the term of your investment and you end up losing money instead of making it, it's easy to berate yourself for having made the wrong decision. But that's only one option. You can also choose to use what you learnt from the experience to guide your next investment decision.

And, it's not just money decisions. You can apply hindsight as a helpful tool to improve relationship outcomes, provided you're prepared to learn from your experiences, no matter how disastrous the relationship.

Learning from hindsight is not about wishing you had done things differently. It's about deciding to do things differently going forward with your next relationship or venture. Hindsight is what enables you to change your behaviour so that you get a different outcome and don't simply go on repeating the same mistakes and getting the same outcomes.

Learning through hindsight is a by-product of self-awareness.

Hindsight is a byproduct of self-awareness. You need to review situations as they unfold if you want to benefit from hindsight. You need to identify and question your assumptions. You need to own your part in whatever went wrong and spend time exploring the lessons the situation is making available for you.

Hindsight allows you to appreciate your mistakes or errors of judgment as lessons you can learn and apply going forward. And, let's face it, we often have to make mistakes to identify the ways that do not work so we can find the ones that do.

Making Space For The Divine

The effective use of hindsight is nothing more than making good use of the feedback available to you.

The least effective use of hindsight is regret - that's basically feeling sorry for yourself instead of looking to learn from whatever the situation has to teach you.

We'd all be better off if we treated hindsight as the gift it can be instead of the curse we often make it.

3 Self-healing practices for busy people

Stop and smell the roses before you burn yourself out.

With the pressures of modern living, it's easy to feel overwhelm - that sense of too much going on in your life.

You've no doubt come across the saying: "When the going gets tough, the tough get going."

That might be true for the tough, but it might not be true for you.

It certainly isn't true for me. In my experience, I make better progress under tough conditions when I choose to look after myself by pausing before I re-enter the fray.

I learnt that the hard way.

Three practices for taming the overwhelm monster.

1. Sitting in silence

Making Space For The Divine

Gift yourself a daily practice of twenty minutes sitting in silence.

Just giving yourself permission to spend time with yourself doing nothing allows you to start seeing things in perspective.

There are two types of silence: external and internal.

Start with external silence. That will allow you the opportunity to hear the thoughts flowing through your mind. You might be surprised by what's going on in there if you give yourself the opportunity to find out.

Don't fight your thoughts, just observe them. Notice what you're telling yourself over and over. Decide if you want to listen or let those thoughts go.

When you're comfortable sitting in a silent space, transition to sitting in silence without entertaining any thoughts.

Internal silence is not as easy to find as external silence. You'll probably find it easier if you join a meditation group and learn to meditate.

2. Listening to music

Some of us find it challenging to sit in silence. Listening to music can be a way into silence, especially if you listen to relaxing instrumental music or songs/chants sung in a language you do not understand.

Listening to music is a way of quietening the mind which has been used as a portal into other dimensions since ancient times. It's a good way to wind down after a busy day.

3. Nature bathing

When life gets tough, get out into nature instead of rushing headlong into those tough circumstances.

Spending time doing nothing surrounded by trees or watching waves crashing onto a shoreline somehow revitalises our depleted inner resources and makes it easier to deal with those tough circumstances.

There is nothing magic about these practices but they will allow miracles into your life - if you let them.

Living alone: An opportunity for self-discovery

For some, living alone is a lifestyle choice. For others, it's an outcome. No matter how you find yourself on your own, it's not a life sentence to loneliness – unless you choose that option.

For your entire life, you live with the best friend you could ever have - yourself.

Many of us live our lives oblivious to that fact, and when we find ourselves on our own, we feel lonely. Some of us actually treat ourselves as the enemy.

It doesn't have to be that way.

One of the possible outcomes of living alone is finding out who you really are. I say one of the possible outcomes deliberately, because there are others, and you need to make a deliberate choice to embark on a journey of self-discovery.

If you are living on your own, I encourage you to make that choice, because the alternatives, like loneliness, depression and alcoholism, are not all that enjoyable. And suicide is final - you don't get to reconsider it after the fact, at least not in this dimension.

The external world is the focus of most of our attempts to understand the world and our place in it. It's true, there is a lot of interesting stuff in the world we can study, and we can keep ourselves busy studying the world for hours. In fact, you can hide there forever if you choose.

The journey of self-discovery, on the other hand, is an inner journey and a very interesting, revealing, and surprising experience, as you encounter yourself along the way. You'll definitely discover you are not who you currently think you are, if you undertake the trip.

To make the journey, you need to turn your focus away from studying things outside yourself and start studying yourself. This journey is about noticing what's going on in your life and wondering why.

Stop wondering why things happened to you. Start wondering why things happened for you to notice. If some things have appeared repeatedly in your life, take notice. You've been missing the lesson.

This journey is not something you'll complete in an afternoon or by attending a weekend workshop. A journey of self-discovery requires commitment to ongoing exploration.

I suggest you start by learning to simply stop and check in with yourself. In my experience, the best way to achieve that is through meditation.

Letting go of things

It's not as easy as you might think.

When sages advise us to give up our attachment to the things of this world to open ourselves to spiritual or personal growth, I suspect most of us think about material things - like people or objects you can actually touch.

When you leave the planet, you leave all your stuff - all the material things - behind. But there are some things we get attached to that are not material - ideas and beliefs.

I'm starting to understand it's ideas and beliefs the sages have in mind when they advise us to let go of our attachments. Whether we take them with us or not, it doesn't take much awareness to realize they influence the way we see things while we are here.

Giving up material things is easy

Our consumer society relies on the fact that it's easy to let go of things. Just consider the size of our landfill problem if you need convincing.

We even have a name for people who can't let their stuff go - hoarders. Extreme hoarding is regarded as a mental illness.

But how many of us are idea or belief hoarders?

How many of us have what are referred to as closed minds? You know - minds that are already made up and not open to anything new - despite the evidence.

We have a term for people in that zone as well - fundamentalists. We usually apply that within a religious context but it can be applied within any context, including science, education, and politics.

Giving up ideas and beliefs is not as easy as giving up things

You could probably give away your watch. But what about the idea of time? Can you allow for eternity or do you want to hold on to linear time with beginnings and endings?

You could probably give away your clothes. But what about your body? Can you give up the belief you're the body and allow for being something else?

You could probably give away the books in your library? But what about the story of your life? Can you give up the belief that your story defines you and allow for new experiences?

Making Space For The Divine

You probably say 'I forgive you' when you want to make peace with someone who has wronged you. But can you let go of the hurt and pain you believe others have caused you to suffer?

You probably say 'I give up' when things don't work out for you. But can you let go of your ten-year plan and allow life to unfold for you?

You probably say 'I know you' when someone close to you says they will change their behaviour. But can you let go of judging and choose to see the divine essence within the person in front of you?

Letting go of what you believe allows you to see the world differently.

Give it a go. It works for me.

Grief and grieving

As we get older, we come to expect the death of elderly parents or relatives, although it's still painful when they die. Their passing is also a reminder that we all get to pass through that portal - no matter what we may believe.

When a person we've known for a long time dies, we grieve the loss of their presence. Simply put, we miss them. When they go, we are left with little more than our memories of the time we spent together.

Digital technology is allowing funeral services to become more of a celebration of the life lived. Fortunately, not everybody needs the over the top coverage a monarch or celebrity gets when they die, but we are starting to do a pretty good job of visually summarising the lives of our loved ones when we gather to farewell them.

My generation is entering their seventies. We have elderly parents approaching death or who have already died. If we're honest with ourselves, we know there is no escape from experiencing the death of our loved ones, just as there is no escape from our own date with the grim reaper. Grief and grieving are common experiences for us now, as not only parents but partners, friends and siblings die around us. After all, death is the destination of every journey that starts with birth, which is why we know it's coming.

When an adult dies, our grief is focussed on the loss of someone we've loved or known for years, perhaps our whole life. Their death creates a gap in the fabric of our story - a gap we feel we have to close. The longer and more intimate the relationship, the bigger and deeper that gap appears to be. Some of us take a long time to recover from the death of a loved one. Some of us never get over it.

The death of a newborn is something else entirely. There is no long relationship that's slowly or suddenly come to an end. There is only a potential relationship that's ended before it had a chance to flower. I think what we grieve when a young child dies, if my experience is anything to go by, is the loss of our hopes and dreams for the child - all the things that could have been if the child had lived.

And, then, there's dealing with the incomprehensible. How do you explain to yourself, let alone to anyone else, the why of such a short, tragic life? From a human perspective, it doesn't make sense for a child to be born only to die a few days or weeks later.

An awareness of the spiritual nature of life allows us a degree of consolation following a death, but we're here to experience life as people living in relationships. And, whether those relationships are lifelong or brief, we need to allow ourselves to feel their loss.

Peter Mulraney

I've come to understand that grief and grieving are outward signs of the vulnerability that allows us to love and be touched by the love of others.

Just as death is part of life, grief is part of the experience of being alive when a loved one dies, so allow yourself to grieve.

A note from Peter

Making Space For The Divine is my fifth book of insights. I hope you enjoy working with the insights and receive a few of your own.

I see sharing these insights, which have come to me over years of meditation and study, as part of my life's work. You can help create a greater awareness of them by writing a review and telling your friends about the book.

You can find details about my other books and read my blog on www.petermulraney.com, where you can subscribe to my monthly newsletter 'Insights from a crime writing mystic' and download a free copy of *A Question of Perspective*.

Get in touch.
www.petermulraney.com

Also by Peter Mulraney

Writings of the Mystic

Sharing the Journey: Reflections of a Reluctant Mystic

My Life is My Responsibility: Insights for Conscious Living

I Am Affirmations: The Power of Words

Beyond the Words: Reflections on I Am Affirmations

Mystical Journey: A Handbook for Modern Mystics

Sharing the Journey Coloring Books

Mandalas

Mandalas by 3

Sharing the Journey Coloring Journals

Sharing the Journey Coloring Journal

Sharing the Journey Coloring Journal ∼Discovery

Sharing the Journey Coloring Journal ∼ Reflection

Crime Fiction

Travers and Palumbo series

Desolation

Distraction

Inspector West series

After

The Holiday

Holy Death

Whistleblower

Twisted Justice

The East Park Syndicate

Inspector West Collection One

Inspector West Collection Two

Stella Bruno Investigates series

The Identity Thief

A Gun of Many Parts

Bones in the Forest

A Deadly Game of Hangman

Taken

Fallout

The Melrose Case

The Scam

Deception

Stella Bruno Investigates: Books 1 to 6

The Identity Thief Collection

The Fallout Collection

The Deception Collection

Ryan Holiday PI Short Stories

Rosie

Framed

Other Fiction

The New Girlfriend

Self-Help

Living Alone series
After She's Gone

Cooking 4 One

Sanity Savers

Living Alone (Collection)

Living Alone Journal

Everyday Business Skills
Everyday Project Management

Everyday Productivity

Everyday Money Management

www.ingramcontent.com/pod-product-compliance
Lightning Source LLC
Chambersburg PA
CBHW030302010526
44107CB00053B/1790